Leadership Skills & Character Building
INTEGRITY & HONESTY

TITLES IN THE SERIES

- Communication Skills
- Initiative, Grit & Perseverance
- Integrity & Honesty
- Organization & Problem-Solving
- Self-Confidence
- Self-Discipline & Responsibility
- Tolerance & Cooperation

Leadership Skills & Character Building

INTEGRITY & HONESTY

Sarah Smith

MASON CREST

Mason Crest
450 Parkway Drive, Suite D
Broomall, Pennsylvania PA 19008
(866) MCP-BOOK (toll free)

First printing
9 8 7 6 5 4 3 2 1

ISBN: 978-1-4222-3997-1
Series ISBN: 978-1-4222-3994-0
ebook ISBN: 978-1-4222-7788-1

Cataloging-in-Publication Data on file with the Library of Congress.

Printed and bound in the United States of America.

QR CODES AND LINKS TO THIRD-PARTY CONTENT

Contents

KEY ICONS TO LOOK FOR:

Words to Understand: These words with their easy-to-understand definitions will increase the reader's understanding of the text while building vocabulary skills.

Sidebars: This boxed material within the main text allows readers to build knowledge, gain insights, explore possibilities, and broaden their perspectives by weaving together additional information to provide realistic and holistic perspectives.

Educational Videos: Readers can view videos by scanning our QR codes, providing them with additional content to supplement the text. Examples include news coverage, moments in history, speeches, iconic sports moments, and much more!

Text-Dependent Questions: These questions send the reader back to the text for more careful attention to the evidence presented there.

Research Projects: Readers are pointed toward areas of further inquiry connected to each chapter. Suggestions are provided for projects that encourage deeper research and analysis.

Series Glossary of Key Terms: This back-of-the-book glossary contains terminology used throughout the series. Words found here increase the reader's ability to read and comprehend higher-level books and articles in this field.

INTRODUCTION: INSPIRATION TO THE READER

The most effective leaders have a combination of intellectual intelligence (IQ), technical skills, and emotional intelligence (EI). Emotional intelligence is an essential ingredient. EI is the act of knowing, understanding, and responding to emotions, overcoming stress in the moment, and being aware of how your words and actions affect others. Emotional intelligence consists of five attributes: self-awareness, self-management, empathy, motivation, and effective communication.

The Unrelenting Athlete

"I've missed more than 9000 shots in my career. I've lost almost 300 games. Twenty-six times I've been trusted to take the game winning shot and missed. I've failed over and over and over again in my life. And that is why I succeed."
—Michael Jordan

The Bold Poets

"I've learned that people will forget what you said, people will forget what you did, but people will never forget how you made them feel."
—Maya Angelou

"What's money? A man is a success if he gets up in the morning and goes to bed at night and in between does what he wants to do."
—Bob Dylan

Becoming more confident as a leader in any capacity will help you inspire others and set a positive example. Gaining confidence in yourself, and finding more joy and peace of mind as you go about life, will help you handle all the successes, challenges, and setbacks along the way. Inside the pages of this book we will discuss all the components to improving your leadership skills, bringing you more confidence and building your character to become the leader you want to be some day.

The Inspiring Creators

"Whether you think you can or you think you can't, you're right."
—Henry Ford

"Strive not to be a success, but rather to be of value."
—Albert Einstein

The Captivating Writer

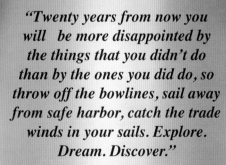

"Twenty years from now you will be more disappointed by the things that you didn't do than by the ones you did do, so throw off the bowlines, sail away from safe harbor, catch the trade winds in your sails. Explore. Dream. Discover."
—Mark Twain

Words to Understand

considerate: thinking about the rights and feelings of other people

culture: the habits, beliefs, and traditions of a particular people

responsible: able to be trusted to do what is right or to do the things that are expected or required

People with integrity and morality understand the need to spend time with older relatives who may need company, or help with day-to-day tasks.

Chapter One
HOW INTEGRITY & HONESTY CAN BUILD LEADERSHIP & CHARACTER

Almost every **culture** around the world shares certain values and tries to instill them in their children. Values are like ideas or standards of behavior that are deemed important and necessary. Among the most essential and timeless ones are honesty and integrity. These character traits are at the heart of what it means to be a "good" person, which includes being **considerate** toward others, true to oneself, **responsible**, tactful, and able to lead—whether in the home, in school, on the sports field, or in the workplace.

What to Expect From This Book

This book should be seen as a thorough study and actionable guide on how to foster more honesty and integrity. Why does this matter? Because these two traits, among others, will have a significant influence on not only the opportunities a person gets in life but also on the quality of their life and relationships, too.

Considered to be some of the most important virtues, honesty and integrity will not just be given lip service here: students will see not only why they are so important, but how they can be developed over time. First, the definitions of integrity and honesty will be explained in detail. Students will be given specific examples showing why having these traits is so beneficial to the individual, as well as the community to which the individual belongs. To contrast the clear benefits of being honest and having integrity, this book will also discuss the downsides of dishonesty. Readers will gain an insight into the

SPEAK WITH
HONESTY
THINK WITH
SINCERITY
ACT WITH
INTEGRITY

Poverty to Wealth: Abraham Lincoln

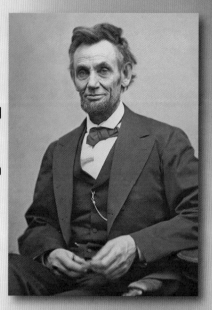

Remembered by his nickname, "Honest Abe," Abraham Lincoln was the sixteenth president of the United States, serving from 1861–1865 during a time of great unrest in America. He led the country through the Civil War and played a major role in reuniting the nation and abolishing slavery.

Before becoming president, Lincoln also studied to become a lawyer and even served as a member of the US Congress in the 1840s. Before that, he earned his way by working as a store clerk as a young man, which is when his nickname Honest Abe got started. Once, he reportedly short-changed a customer by accident and then closed the shop so he could walk to the customer's home and deliver the correct change.

The high value that he placed on integrity and honesty earned him the respect of his peers and constituents. His sincerity and fairness helped him become one of history's greatest leaders. One of his closest friends, a lawyer by the name of Leonard Swett, said of him: "He believed in the great laws of truth, the right discharge of duty, his accountability to God, the ultimate triumph of the right, and the overthrow of wrong."

detrimental effects of lying and deceit, which go far beyond the obvious consequence of hurt feelings.

Readers will then learn about how they can use the traits of honesty and integrity to improve the relationships they have with others, especially their friends, family members, and colleagues. They'll explore the broad yet useful concept of "being likable" and learn how to present their best self to the world.

This issue of being likable is extremely important to the teen and young adult, who is in an important life period of self-development and empowerment. Students will see how caring about the traits of honesty and integrity can help them avoid harmful behaviors such as illicit drug and alcohol use, no matter how difficult it can feel to avoid these temptations when trying to "fit in."

Ultimately, true honesty and integrity require a deep level of self-respect and self-love. Students will wrap up their learning by understanding how greater self-respect can increase a person's honesty and integrity, and vice versa—how aiming to be more honest and have more integrity in day-to-day life can increase a person's sense of self-worth and self-respect.

And, oh, how this matters, because the true leaders of the future (on local and global scales), who will be able to make a significant difference in this world, are the ones who believe in themselves enough to do it.

So let's get started!

Text-Dependent Questions

1. What are "values?"

2. Why are those who have integrity and honesty less likely to take illicit drugs?

3. Why was Abraham Lincoln able earn respect from his peers and constituents?

Research Project

Have you ever let someone take the blame for something you did, or have you failed to keep a promise, or gossiped about a good friend? Explain why all of these actions show a lack of integrity.

Words to Understand

ethical: following accepted rules of behavior; morally right and good

honesty: free of untruthfulness; sincere

integrity: the quality of being honest and having strong moral principles; moral uprightness

This photograph shows a group of people doing a cleanup after a flood. They have volunteered in order to help the community and are pleased to do so. Even though others have not offered to help, this group is showing integrity by getting on with the job in hand regardless.

Chapter Two
THE BENEFITS OF INTEGRITY & HONESTY

M̲ost people have a good idea of what it means to be honest:

Tell the truth.
Don't steal, lie, or cheat.
Play fair.

Integrity is closely related. To have **integrity**, a person must be willing to be honest with themselves and with others about their feelings, desires, needs, fears, and thoughts. People who have integrity are known for being fair, **ethical**, and respectful.

In other words, integrity is like **honesty** in action. It's often described this way: *Doing the right thing, even when no one is watching.*

Greenpeace is an organization that works to protect the natural environment. It has millions of members who feel that it is morally and ethically right to protect the planet.

The Benefits of Integrity & Honesty

But this begs an important question: How is one supposed to know what the "right" thing is, especially when faced with a difficult choice? This is when a person's honesty and integrity truly play an important role.

A Quotation to Ponder
"You are what you do, not what you say you'll do."
—C. G. Jung, Swiss psychologist

Being Honest Helps You Make Decisions: Four Questions to Ask Yourself When Making a Tough Choice

People must make difficult choices all the time: where to go to college, when to accept or leave a job, when to end a relationship, and so on. Honestly answering the following four questions (based on the work of American psychotherapist Alison Thayer) can help a person make the right choice in any given circumstance. Note, however, that often there is more than one right choice. The goal, then, is for every person to make the *best possible* right choice for them, based on their personal values, beliefs, goals, and needs. Remember, too, that the right choice is also one that does not hurt or infringe on the rights of someone else.

1. What Are the Pros & Cons of Each Possible Choice I Have?
This question helps a person gain clarity about their situation while also stimulating creative problem-solving.

Living with integrity

In almost all situations, telling the truth is by far the best option, as the more honest a person is, the more likely he or she will be respected by others.

2. How Would This Decision Affect Me or Others in the Future (E.g., One Year From Now)?

This question helps a person think about the long-term consequences of a choice and teaches the value of patience.

3. What Would Be the Worst-Case Scenario & How Could I Prepare for That?

This question helps someone identify and prepare for potential factors that may affect the outcome of a decision, thus reducing anxiety. After all, even the worst-case scenario isn't usually all that bad. Reflecting on it beforehand can help a person avoid unnecessary worrying that would otherwise distract them from making the "right" choice.

4. What Advice Would I Give Someone Else About This Decision?

People tend to be overly critical about themselves but more generous and kindhearted toward others. People also tend to give the advice they want to hear. This question can help a person look at their problem from the point of view of a caring friend rather than a harsh critic.

The Benefits of Integrity & Honesty

Tell the Truth: It's Good for Your Health!

Research from 2012 conducted at the University of Notre Dame found that people who lie less tend to have better mental health (e.g., fewer complaints of stress and tension), as well as better physical health (e.g., fewer complaints of illness and chronic pain).

Bill Gates is the founder of Microsoft. As a philanthropist and humanitarian, he took pride in running his business with integrity as honesty. Today, Bill and his wife, Melinda, chair the Gates Foundation, the world's largest private charitable foundation. The foundation works to save lives and improve the health of people all over the world.

More Honesty Equals Better Outcomes

Notice that the above questions all require an individual to take an honest, creative, and introspective look at himself or herself. This is key.

Why? Because while so many things can affect the outcome of a personal decision, not all of these things can be controlled. This includes factors such as the weather, the stock market, the economy, and other people's actions, thoughts, or feelings.

With this in mind, good decision-makers (and good leaders) use deliberate and thoughtful insight to help them problem-solve. It helps them recognize the difference between things they can control and things they can't; that way, they can focus their energy appropriately. This may take a little more time, but this additional time is helpful since it can prevent someone from making impulsive choices based solely on emotion instead of logic and reason.

The more honest and practical a person can be during the decision-making process, the more likely it is they will get their desired outcomes. And even if an outcome doesn't turn out the way they want, it's the honest and truthful people who can handle their setbacks and get back on their feet more efficiently.

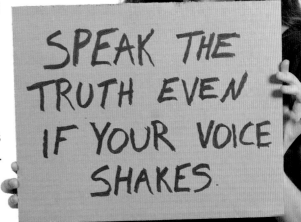

Top Benefits to Approaching School, Work, Relationships & Life With Honesty and Integrity

We just learned that one of the most significant benefits of honesty and integrity is that these

The Benefits of Integrity & Honesty

qualities can help a person be a more effective problem-solver. There are several other key benefits as well, which can translate into positive outcomes within school, work, relationships, and more:

- Being honest teaches a person how to be in control of their emotions.
- Being honest helps a person feel empowered and self-loving.
- Being honest helps a person cultivate the courage to do the "right" thing, even when it's scary or uncomfortable.
- Being honest helps a person feel free to be who they are, which can attract people into their life who will accept and love them for who they are.
- Being honest (and acting with integrity) helps a person avoid uncomfortable and often troublesome consequences of *dishonest* behavior such as lying, breaking the law, stealing, etc.

Would you consider yourself to be a truthful and honest person? Do you feel it is important to do the "right" thing? Striving for these qualities will improve the quality of your personal and work life.

- Being honest promotes deeper and more loving connections with others and promotes harmony, cooperation, and teamwork.
- Being honest helps a person be a role model and helps encourage other people to be honest, too.

Psychological research shows that being honest and telling the truth isn't just about being a "goody two-shoes" or a teacher's pet. By being honest, children and young adults are setting themselves up for more success in all areas of their lives.

Notice that the benefits of an individual being honest extend beyond just that one person. *Other* people benefit from a person's willingness to be fair, ethical, honest, and truthful, too! In this way, young students who challenge themselves to act with more honesty and integrity have the potential to make a big positive impact on their friends, family, classmates, and even future colleagues and community members.

Text-Dependent Questions

1. What does it mean to have integrity?

2. Name two benefits of being honest.

3. How does honesty affect decision-making?

Research Project

When you think about honesty, who comes to mind? You've already learned that Abraham Lincoln was known for being an honest and ethical man. Spend about 30 to 45 minutes researching another famous historical person who was known for having integrity and being honest. Then, write a brief one- to two-page summary about their life, including their contributions and any specific examples of how their honesty and integrity helped them, their life mission, and others around them.

Words to Understand

plagiarism: the practice of taking someone else's work or ideas and passing them off as one's own

remorse: deep regret or guilt for a wrong committed

white lie: a harmless or trivial lie, especially one told to avoid hurting someone's feeling

Being told a lie makes you feel uncomfortable to say the least, but at worst can make you feel sad or angry. Even white lies, used to protect another's feelings, should only be used when really necessary.

Chapter Three
THE DETRIMENTAL EFFECTS OF DISHONESTY

How many of us lie?

Research varies, but it's been estimated that the typical person lies an average of two times per day. Of course, this doesn't mean that the typical person is a "bad" person. It simply points to the fact that lying and dishonesty are a typical part of many cultures around the world. It could even be argued that they're a typical part of human nature.

But how much and what kind of dishonesty should be considered okay?

The Good & the Bad of the "Little White Lie"

Probably the most common, everyday usage of dishonesty is with the so-called little **white lie**. White lies are typically seen as harmless statements, despite not being entirely truthful. They are often told as a way to avoid hurting someone else's feelings. For instance, when someone asks, "Are my teeth yellow?" or, "Did I gain weight over winter break?" the other person may be tempted not to say what's really on their mind, and instead modify their response so the person asking the question isn't offended or insulted.

While this can be seen as an act of consideration for the other person's feelings, it also could be argued that the person's honest opinion may actually be beneficial to the person asking for it. It could inspire someone to make a healthy change, for instance, such as flossing more or cutting out sugar from their diet.

Do As I Say, Not As I Do?

Researchers from the University of Toronto in Canada found that even parents who teach their children that honesty is important still lie to them from time to time. The same researchers suggest that this can cause mixed signals for children and disrupt the parent/child bond.

The Detrimental Effects of Dishonesty

There are times when all of us will need to deliver bad news that may hurt someone's feelings or upset them in some other way. To make the situation less stressful, if at all possible, speak to the person tactfully and truthfully. Do not be tempted to tell a white lie to soften the situation.

The bottom line is that while it's reasonable to say that almost everyone will tell a little white lie now and then, it's wise to avoid making it a habit—yes, even the white lies. When a young person notices themselves telling a white lie, they should use it as a cue to later ask themselves a few questions that may help them gain greater insight into their own behavior. Consider questions such as:

- Why did I just feel the need to lie?
- How could I have spoken my truthful answer in a polite way?
- If I were in their shoes, would I want to know the other person's honest opinion?

These questions are a great way to develop the habit of honesty while still showing respect and thoughtfulness for others.

Four Ways That Dishonesty Can Affect Your Life

Unfortunately, lying seems very easy to do, and people of all ages will lie for many different reasons. From trying to look good, to fear of punishment, to trying to gain an unfair advantage, the reasons people lie (and how often they do it) will vary significantly.

To help break the habit of lying and dishonesty, it's helpful to reflect on the specific downsides of lying. Note that many downsides can still occur even if the person doesn't get caught!

1. Dishonesty Can Impair the Quality of Your Schoolwork
Dishonesty in school (or poor academic integrity) can lead to severe consequences

Cheating at school is dishonest and pointless. The consequences can range from getting detention or having college acceptances taken back.

The Detrimental Effects of Dishonesty

for the student. These consequences can range from getting detention to even having college acceptances taken back. But academic dishonesty goes way beyond getting in trouble with the teacher. Students who are dishonest (for instance, by copying their friends' homework or cheating during an exam) will probably not learn as much about the subject as someone else who works hard at it.

A Quotation to Ponder
"Accuracy is the twin brother of honesty; inaccuracy, of dishonesty."

—Nathaniel Hawthorne, American novelist

Plagiarism, or the act of taking someone else's work and passing it off as one's own, is one of the more serious examples of academic dishonesty. Most schools,

To avoid plagiarism, be sure to give proper credit where credit's due.

How to tell if
someone is lying
to you

colleges, and universities typically have strict academic integrity policies as well as specific guidelines on how their institution deals with cases of **plagiarism.** Historically, students have failed courses, lost scholarships, and have even been expelled because of this type of dishonest behavior.

It's important to realize that a person can even plagiarize accidentally. This often happens when a student fails to properly give credit where credit's due. You can avoid this by taking steps such as using a bibliography in a report, using a hyperlink in an online blog post, or using quotation marks and giving the original source's name.

2. Repeatedly Lying to Yourself or Others Can Put You at Risk for Physical & Mental Health Problems

As mentioned, even if a person isn't caught for lying, the very act of lying can lead to mental health concerns such as anxiety and depression. Research has shown this is related to a psychological concept known as "cognitive dissonance." This term refers to the emotional and mental discomfort experienced when a person's actions do not match that person's beliefs. In other words, if a person believes that telling the truth is fair and decent, but then lies to their boss about why they were late for work, this person may end up feeling stressed-out and distracted. Not only can this distraction impair a person's health but it also may impair their productivity and quality of work on the job, for instance.

3. Lying Can Break Down Trust Within a Relationship & Cause Loved Ones to Grow Resentful

This will be discussed in greater detail in the following chapter. For now, it's helpful

The Detrimental Effects of Dishonesty

to remember that repeatedly lying or hiding the truth from someone often leads to conflict with that person. It is most people's experience that being lied to is unpleasant and can lead to hurt feelings. Good leaders, and anyone who wants to build healthy and loving relationships with other people, inherently understand that other people deserve their honesty and truthfulness.

4. Being Dishonest Can Get You In Trouble With the Law
In addition to plagiarism, other acts of dishonesty (such as stealing, tax evasion, and fraud) often come with legal ramifications. This means that the justice system can find a person guilty of their dishonest act and enforce consequences, such as fines or even jail time.

Stealing is wrong on any level. This girl is shoplifting, which can lead to a criminal record.

The Upside to Remorse

Usually, when people tell lies, they end up feeling badly about it later. If a person wants to break their habit of being dishonest, it can actually be helpful to have emotions like guilt and **remorse**. Such painful and difficult emotions are like tools that can help a person stop and think about the choices they have made and prevent them from making the same errors in the future.

Good leaders are good at doing this—that is, learning how to use their emotions as tools to help them learn about and improve upon themselves. A good leader is able to own up to their mistakes, take responsibility for their actions, and handle the consequences of their occasional mistakes with grace and humility.

Text-Dependent Questions

1. Name two ways in which being dishonest can negatively affect aspects of your daily life.

2. Name two or three signs that may indicate someone is lying to you.

3. Why might feeling guilty after telling a lie be a good thing?

Research Project

Do some research on plagiarism. Then write a two- to three-page report explaining in more detail about what you've learned. Include information such as what plagiarism is, examples of plagiarism, and how plagiarism can be avoided. The following website should help you as you do your research: http://www.plagiarism.org/article/what-is-plagiarism.

Words to Understand

acquaintance: a person one knows slightly, but who is not a close friend

gossip: casual or unconstrained conversation or reports about other people, typically involving details that are not confirmed as being true

trustworthy: deserving faith and confidence

Having a good relationship with your parents will make you less likely to rebel as a teenager. Listen to their advice as they have a wealth of experience that can be passed on to you.

Chapter Four
IMPROVING RELATIONSHIPS
WITH FRIENDS & FAMILY

Relationships are extremely important to health. Research even shows that things like money and success are less meaningful and rewarding if healthy close bonds with other people are missing. People with quality relationships also tend to have fewer health problems and greater subjective happiness in life.

But whether relationships are solid or rocky, old or new, deeply intimate or more of an **acquaintance**, they take work. It's wise to never take someone for granted: giving extra attention and care to friends and family is a great way to get more satisfaction, fulfillment, and enjoyment out of life.

Having good friends in your peer group is an important part of growing up. Very often, friends that are made while you are young will stay your friends for life.

Want to Live Longer? Get Some Good Buddies!

According to Harvard Medical School, research has shown that a lack of strong relationships can increase a person's risk of early death by as much as 50 percent. This is as bad as smoking!

A Quotation to Ponder
"If you treat people at the end of the relationship like the beginning, there won't be an end."

— Tony Robbins, American motivational speaker, author, and entrepreneur

Those of us who build good and honest relationships with partners, friends, and family are less likely to suffer from mental health problems and there is evidence our physical health is better too.

Ten Insightful Questions That Can Help You Be a Better Friend, Partner, or Family Member

Young people should get in the habit of analyzing the most important relationships in their lives and figuring out how they can help improve these relationships. The following insightful and honest questions can be extremely helpful when trying to become closer and more intimate with a loved one:

- Do I act in accordance with my values? Do my behaviors match my words?
- Do I make excuses? Do I follow through?
- Am I dependable?
- Do I handle and respond to constructive criticism well?
- Do I listen? Do I create a sense of acceptance and caring, or judgment and resentment?
- Am I **trustworthy**? Do I avoid **gossip** and bad-mouthing? Do I keep secrets?
- Do I express my concerns and needs in an effective and loving way?
- Do I lie? When and why?
- Do I embrace this person's "negative" sides as well as their "positive" sides?
- Do I take responsibility for my mistakes in the relationship? Do I apologize?

Even as little as twenty to thirty minutes reflecting on these questions in a journal or Word document can help a person gain incredible insight into their role as a friend or loved one.

Tips for a healthier relationship

Helping an elderly relative is a rewarding experience and can be enjoyable, too. Older people invariably have a wealth of knowledge and experience that can be very interesting to the younger generation.

Remember: people want to be treated with respect, kindness, and understanding. It's a strange habit of many people to treat strangers with more respect and politeness than their own partners, family members, or closest friends. And while nobody should expect to never have conflict with loved ones, it's important for the sake of a relationship to practice the habit of acting with honesty, grace, and generosity. Even a little bit goes a long way.

Text-Dependent Questions

1. Why is it good for you to have happy relationships with others?

2. What is gossip?

3. Why should you treat people with respect and kindness?

Research Project

Take a few moments to identify a relationship in your life that currently seems to have a lot of conflict. Maybe you're at odds with your sibling or not communicating well with a parent. Maybe you're fighting with your best friend or not working effectively with a teammate. Using the ten suggested questions listed above, spend twenty to thirty minutes reflecting on how you are contributing to the current state of the relationship. Be honest with yourself. Of course the other person is contributing to the quality (or lack of quality) of the relationship, too. But can you identify and accept responsibility for *your* impact? At the end of your self-reflection, try writing a letter to your loved one. You don't have to give it to him or her (though you're more than welcome to), but sometimes the simple act of "speaking" to the other person can bring a great sense of peace, forgiveness, acceptance, and understanding within you.

Words to Understand

authentic: genuine; true to one's self

rapport: a close and harmonious relationship in which the people or groups concerned understand each other's feelings or ideas and communicate well

Subordinate: to treat or regard as of lesser importance than something else

Being truly likable requires some important qualities including being considerate and kind while still being true to oneself.

Chapter Five
BEING LIKABLE

Every person has something unique to offer this world: different strengths, different insights, different experiences, different skills, and different beliefs. And here's another thing humans have in common: Just about everyone wants to be loved and appreciated for who they are.

After all, it feels good to get to know others, open up to trustworthy people, and develop caring and respectful relationships.

To do all this—to enjoy the gifts of friendship—it's helpful to be considered a likable person. But being likable isn't just about trying to "fit in." Being truly likable and pleasant to be around means being able to be considerate and kind while *still* being true to oneself, and expressing oneself freely and honestly.

A Quotation to Ponder
"Don't wait for people to be friendly; show them how."
—Unknown

Being likable ultimately comes down to having good social awareness. The socially aware person (considered "emotionally intelligent" by many researchers) can understand how other people feel. This understanding helps promote trust and cooperation, which can benefit everyone involved.

Top Dos & Don'ts for Presenting Your Best Self

People are highly social by nature, which makes friendship-building an extremely important part of the collective human experience. To avoid "rubbing people the wrong way" and help improve your relationship-building skills, consider the following dos and don'ts:

DON'T Ignore Body Language
When meeting someone for the first time, or interacting with a friend, colleague, or respected authority figure (such as a teacher, coach, or boss), it's important to

Being Likable

Nonverbal communication (also known as body language) has an influence on what kind of impression a person makes on someone else. While this girl is giving her friend a hug, her facial expression suggests she isn't as warm-hearted as she first would appear to her friend.

Good friends or bad friends

smile, make eye contact, leave one's arms relaxed by the side, and avoid fidgeting. Nonverbal communication (also known as body language) will have a huge influence on what kind of impression a person makes on someone else.

It's worth remembering that different societies have different cultural expectations for body language. For instance, some cultures find it rude to look someone in the eye. Any young person who hopes to serve a leadership role on a community, national, or global scale should be prepared to learn about the different cultures they interact with and to not be afraid to ask questions either. This shows respect, tactfulness, and maturity.

DON'T Subordinate Yourself Just to Please Someone Else
The tactful and intelligent person is someone who can communicate what they need or desire, state their opinions, and stand up for what they believe in without

In a business environment, personality traits such as sincerity, understanding, and transparency are considered to be very important when assessing a person's likability.

Being Likable

When in a discussion with another person, it is good manners to listen to what the other person has to say and make eye contact with them while they are speaking. Looking bored or indifferent will make the person you are with feel uncomfortable.

Making an effort to remember and use someone's name during a conversation will instantly give the good impression that you are an attentive and genuine person.

putting someone else down. Nobody likes to be told what to do or listen to someone who comes off like a know-it-all. At the same time, it doesn't feel good or honorable to simply agree with someone just because of some need to please or impress that person.

Likable people aren't afraid to be who they are. But at the same time, they allow other people to be who *they* are, too.

DO Use People's Names
Using someone's name at least one or two times per conversation is a great way to build **rapport** and create a friendly and inviting impression on others. This is especially important when meeting someone for the first time or going to a job interview.

DO Try to See Things From Another Person's Perspective
No two people have the exact same beliefs. By trying to walk a mile in someone

Being Likable

Does Likability Matter in the Workplace?

According to a 2015 study at the University of California, Los Angeles, the most important personality traits of people considered likable by their peers include things like sincerity, transparency, and understanding. What's interesting to note is that these traits have more to do with social interaction rather than innate characteristics. This is why the same people surveyed placed slightly less importance on traits like attractiveness and intelligence when it comes to deciding if someone is likable or not.

Being a good listener will make you more likable and able to see the world through the eyes of others. It will also enrich your understanding and capacity for empathy.

else's shoes, it can be much easier to communicate needs in a likable, effective, and cooperative way.

To help see things from other people's perspectives, ask meaningful questions about their lives, thoughts, and feelings—and then truly *listen* to their answers. Instead of interrupting, or just waiting to speak, be present and listen to what the person is saying. If it's not clear, ask clarifying follow-up questions. People who are good listeners tend to be seen as more likable and friendly by others, which can bring many unique opportunities within school, the workplace, or social settings.

DO Take the Time & Space to Simply Observe

People watching is a great way to hone one's own social awareness skills. By simply sitting quietly at a library, mall, or park bench, a person can learn a lot from politely observing other people as they go about their day.

By sitting quietly on a park bench you can observe the people around you. A person can learn a lot from politely observing other people as they go about their day.

Being Likable

Creating space to notice and observe things about other people can also happen within individual conversations.

Being Likable Starts With Liking YOURSELF

Being well liked makes people feel good, and, in the grand scheme of things, being popular is probably far less important than developing genuine relationships with people who allow one another to be their **authentic** selves.

Many teens will go through a stage in life where they lack self-confidence and this can lead to negative thoughts about their own likability. Learning to love yourself will increase your confidence and help you to form good friendships and relationships.

It is also important to appreciate, that people can only form good relationships if they have learned to love themselves as well as others. This will be touched on in greater detail in the final chapter on self-respect. In the meantime, it's worthwhile to remember that age-old wisdom: *You can only love others as much as you love yourself.* In other words, if a person wants to be more likable and have more friends, then he or she needs to start treating *themselves* like their own friend! People who like themselves shine with confidence, warm-heartedness, and good-natured energy, and naturally attract others into their lives.

Text-Dependent Questions

1. What does social awareness mean?

2. List three characteristics of a good friend and three characteristics of a bad friend.

3. Why is it an advantage to be a good listener?

Research Project

Spend about thirty to sixty minutes researching "emotional intelligence." This is a key psychological concept and is closely related to the issues of likability, authenticity, integrity, and overall success in life. After your research, write a one- to three-page report on what you've learned, including what emotional intelligence is, any famous pioneers or researchers involved, and whether (and how) you can increase your emotional intelligence.

Words to Understand

illicit: forbidden by law, rules, or custom

peer pressure: influence from members of one's peer group

peer: a person of the same age, status, or ability as another specified person

Drugs and alcohol are bad for your health and, while most of us know this, there are times when some people are tempted by many factors, including peer pressure. The best policy is to always say "No!"

Chapter Six
AVOIDING DRUGS, ALCOHOL & TOBACCO

So far, this book has talked a lot about how being honest not only feels good but can actually be good for one's health. This book has also pointed out how the consequences of dishonesty and a lack of integrity (in other words, not doing the right thing) can lead to mental and physical stress, let alone potential problems in relationships, school, the workplace, or even with the law. For teens and young adults, one of the most common struggles of "doing the right thing" is avoiding drugs, tobacco, and cigarettes.

People know drugs and alcohol aren't good for health. But despite this general knowledge, it remains a common issue for people of all ages, let alone teens and young adults.

Some of this has to do with addiction: the very nature of nicotine, alcohol, and **illicit** drugs means that they tend to be habit-forming or addictive, which can make it extremely difficult to stop using them. But aside from the potentially addictive qualities of drugs there's also usually a few other factors at play, including **peer pressure**.

Honesty & Integrity: Tools for Standing Up to Peer Pressure

This book has already shown readers how being honest to others and being true to one's self can help make a person more likable. Unfortunately, another common way people try to be liked by others is by giving in to peer pressure.

Peer pressure is real, but that doesn't necessarily make it right. Nobody should feel forced to "give in" and compromise their values in order to be friends with someone. Plus, the short-term pain and embarrassment of saying no to illegal substances is almost always far less significant than the long-term pleasure of the confidence and heightened self-worth one gets by staying true to themselves.

Honesty is the best policy when it comes to saying no to drugs or alcohol. Be polite, but firm. Anyone who has a problem with someone saying no to drugs or alcohol probably just has a problem with themselves and is taking it out on the other person, whose integrity may make them feel guilty or badly about their own

Avoiding Drugs, Alcohol & Tobacco

Don't be tempted to socialize with people who smoke, take illicit drugs, or drink alcohol. Pressures from a peer group can be very strong and before long, you could become embroiled in similar behavior. It is best to mix with a group who have healthier pastimes.

Is It Really Worth It?

According to the US Centers for Disease Control and Prevention (CDC), as many as 4,300 kids and teens under the age of twenty-one die every year because of excessive alcohol use. In Canada, about this many people of all ages die due to excessive alcohol consumption, according to a 2015 report by the Chief Public Health Officer.

poor decisions. But while everyone deserves compassion and understanding (including drug and alcohol users), certain people might need to be turned down, simply for your own physical, mental, and emotional well-being.
Besides, saying no doesn't have to be embarrassing anyway!

Five Ways to Say No to Alcohol & Drugs

1. Someone says: *"Everybody's doing it. It's not a big deal."* Try saying: **Tons of people don't do drugs/drink alcohol. Besides, I just don't want to.**

2. Someone says: *"Just try it. It'll make you feel good."* Try saying: **I already feel pretty good. Thanks anyway.**

3. Someone says: *"If we're gonna be friends, you have to drink/get high with me."* Try saying: **You know, I like *you*, not the drugs/alcohol.**

4. Someone says: *"Come on, no one will know."* Try saying: **I'll know. Plus, I don't want to take any chances. I'd get in so much trouble if I got caught.**

SAY No TO DRUGS

Avoiding Drugs, Alcohol & Tobacco

How to not drink: dealing with peer pressure

If you are offered any drug, you should always refuse it. The chemicals in it could be extremely dangerous or even kill you.

5. Someone says: "*It's cool.*" Try saying: **I know people who have gotten really sick doing that. Kinda uncool if you ask me.**

Of course, never forget the most simple and straightforward response: "No thanks!" Try saying it with a smile!

Even if the honest person prepares a few polite ways to say no ahead of time, it can still feel uncomfortable (especially if someone has to say no to a friend). So anyone who truly wants to avoid the negative consequences of participating in underage drinking or illegal drug use may simply decide to avoid putting him or herself in situations where that type of behavior is common (like at parties).

Does this mean it's "uncool" to act with integrity and honesty and decline an invite to that Friday night party? Of course not. It's *always* cool to make healthier choices for oneself, such as avoiding drugs and alcohol, drunk driving, unsafe sex, and other inappropriate behaviors. Plus, in a world where

Vaping was once designed to help people give up cigarettes, however, e-cigarettes are themselves addictive. Many of the harmful chemicals found in traditional cigarettes are completely missing from e-cigarettes. On the flip side, e-cigarettes are relatively new and little research into their long-term effects has been carried out.

Saying No to Cigarettes, E-Cigarettes & Vaping? You're Not Alone!

According to US government data, the rate of youth tobacco use is the lowest it's ever been. At last, it seems that kids and teens in the US are finally starting to understand just how gross this habit really is! It is also worth noting that e-cigarettes and vaping are not without health risks.

Avoiding Drugs, Alcohol & Tobacco

When meeting with friends, try to opt for an occasion that doesn't involve alcohol or cigarettes. This is a good habit to get into, as the regular use of alcohol and cigarettes is not good for health.

college acceptance and the job market (even the start-up/entrepreneurial route) are more competitive than ever, it's easy to imagine how much of an advantage a young person has who stays home, works on their studies or hobbies, takes care of their health, and stays out of trouble compared to someone who abuses their body with drugs and alcohol—and who has to deal with a hangover the next day!

It's always possible to join a group of friends who share the same values of staying drug- and alcohol-free. And remember: We only get one body. The more respect and care we give to our health, the more we can get out of life.

Text-Dependent Questions

1. About how many young people die every year in America due to excessive alcohol drinking?

2. What does peer pressure mean?

3. Why is saying "No!" to drugs cool?

Research Project

Time to get creative! Come up with between ten and twenty possible responses of your own for how to politely say no if you're ever offered drugs or alcohol. Remember, honesty is the best policy. Don't feel like you have to make up any sort of elaborate story explaining why you don't want to join in. A simple "No thank you" is more than good enough!

Words to Understand

arrogant: having an exaggerated sense of one's own importance or abilities

Flattery: excessive and insincere praise, especially that given to further one's own interests

Self-respect: pride and confidence in oneself; a feeling that one is behaving with honor and dignity

Self-respect is essential to living a happy and fulfilling life.

Chapter Seven
SELF-RESPECT

The world, as many philosophers and poets say, is like a mirror. It reflects back what a person feels about themselves. In this sense, the more respect and self-love a person has for himself or herself, the more he or she can give respect and love to the important people in their life, too, which can translate into better relationships with others *and* with the self.

Self-respect is also essential to living an honest, successful, and fulfilling life. Fortunately, by acting with integrity, being honest, and being true to one's self, a person can become more self-loving over time.

A Quotation to Ponder
"A man sees in the world what he carries in his heart."
— Johann Wolfgang von Goethe, German polymath

Five Signs of a Person With a Good Sense of Self-Respect

It's never too late to start treating oneself with more love and kindness (the same way anyone would want their loved ones treated!). The following ten characteristics and traits are often found in people who identify as having a high degree of self-respect. Students can use these models as a way to track their own progress toward living in a more honest and authentic way:

1. They Accept Themselves, Including Their So-Called Faults
American psychology professor Dr. Kristin Neff has done a lot of work on the concept of self-compassion, which is related to self-respect. According to her research and other studies, being compassionate toward oneself (in other words, being kind, understanding, and patient) is related to higher levels of happiness, optimism, and overall well-being.

It's important to note that, according to Dr. Neff, a self-compassionate, self-respectful person does not ignore their faults. People with a high degree of self-respect feel that way because they know they are worthy of love and care exactly as they are. They don't just love themselves when they feel good about

The High Cost of Low Self-Esteem

Data from the website www.dosomething.org shows that three-quarters of teen girls who report having low self-esteem participate in unhealthy and risky behaviors like cutting, bullying, unsafe sex, drinking, and smoking. On the other hand, only one-quarter of teen girls who report having high self-esteem participate in these types of behaviors.

Learning and practicing self-compassion is essential if one wants to avoid the downsides that come with low self-esteem. And this even applies to people who currently have good self-esteem because life is unpredictable and they can sometimes lose their confidence, too.

themselves. They love themselves even when they make mistakes or show faults. This also helps them take responsibility for their actions and truly learn from their mistakes.

2. They Do Not Tolerate Unhealthy Relationships
People who are honest about what they want out of life will not settle for a partner who does not treat them with respect and kindness. They don't compromise on what truly matters just to please someone else. Because they don't depend on another person to make them feel complete and whole, self-respectful people are able to politely yet firmly leave a relationship when it is no longer serving them. They can say no without feeling guilty

3. They Treat Their Bodies With Respect
People with a high sense of self-respect understand their bodies are a temporary gift and should be given love and health. They tend to place a high value on health because they know that without good health a person will never be able to get the most out of life.

Accordingly, a person who respects herself will avoid alcohol, drugs, and junk food; will exercise and eat nutritious food; and will practice safer sex, wear seat belts, and practice other preventative, health-conscious behaviors.

4. They Do Not Depend on Criticism or Flattery

A person with a good sense of self-respect gets his sense of self-worth from within. While he can graciously enjoy compliments, he does not depend on them or let them inflate his ego. Equally, while the self-respecting person will listen to and explore criticism, he won't let it get him down or trick him into thinking

It is very important not to tolerate an unhealthy relationship where you feel you are not respected.

he is a failure. Lastly, instead of comparing himself to others, a person with a high degree of self-compassion and respect focuses more on his own personal progress within any given area of life and remains appreciative of what he has.

5. They Are Confident & Believe in Their Abilities and Potential

People who are compassionate and respectful toward themselves are less likely to struggle with anxiety and depression. They are also more likely to have a healthy amount of confidence without being overly **arrogant**, cocky, or self-centered. Confidence is essential for any leader in life who wants to inspire others, make a

10 easy ways to improve your self esteem

change, and fulfill their own potential. Before doing and having what they want, self-respectful people are able to *believe* they can first.

Self-Respect, Integrity & Honesty: Key Ingredients for a Fulfilling Life in a Changing World

The "real world" can be a challenging place. People aren't always honest or even particularly respectful. People often say things, either intentionally or unintentionally, that can lead to hurt feelings and confusion (especially in the modern age of technology and social media, where people can hide behind

The world can be a difficult place for today's teenagers. Social media, in particular, can put pressures on teens that older people never had to experience in days gone past.

computer screens while saying hurtful things they'd never say face-to-face). In some cases, people may even attempt to directly cause another person harm.

In spite of this reality (and maybe even because of it), teaching our younger generations the value of honesty is more necessary than ever. Building a sense of self-respect, acting with integrity, and placing a high value on honesty can truly help any young person navigate the changing world. And whether at school, in the workforce, or in their personal lives, young people who are willing to be honest (with themselves and one another) about their values and beliefs can expect to *feel* empowered, and *be* inspiring.

Text-Dependent Questions

1. List at least three ways in which you can increase your self-esteem.

2. Name two characteristics of someone who tends to have a high degree of self-respect.

3. Why are people more likely to say something disrespectful through social media than when face-to-face with someone.

Research Project

Create a "Pat My Own Back" list. Spend twenty to thirty minutes writing down a list of all the things in life you're proud of, all the accomplishments you've achieved, and all the things you truly love and admire about yourself. Don't say "nothing"! This exercise may feel difficult and uncomfortable, but it is *so* important. Being your own biggest support system (instead of just your own biggest critic) can truly help you learn to love not only yourself but also *others* more fully and openly as well. So go ahead and give yourself a round of applause.

Series Glossary of Key Terms

ability	Power to do something.
addiction	A strong and harmful need to regularly have something (such as a drug).
anxiety	Fear or nervousness about what might happen.
argument	An angry disagreement.
assumption	Something accepted as true.
body language	Movements or positions of the body that express a person's thoughts or feelings.
challenge	A stimulating task or problem.
citizen	A person who lives in a particular place.
clarify	To make or become more easily understood.
collaborate	To work with others.
conclusion	Final decision reached by reasoning.
conflict	A clashing disagreement (as between ideas or interests).
confusion	Difficulty in understanding or in being able to tell one thing from a similar thing.
cooperation	The act or process of working together to get something done.
counsellor	A person who gives advice.
criticism	The act of finding fault.
culture	The habits, beliefs, and traditions of a particular people, place, or time.
discipline	Strict training that corrects or strengthens.
discriminate	To unfairly treat a person or group differently from other people or groups.
efficiency	The ability to do something or produce something without waste.
effort	Hard physical or mental work.
evidence	A sign which shows that something exists or is true.
experience	Skill or knowledge that you get by doing something.
feedback	Helpful criticism given to someone to indicate what can be done to improve something.
frustration	A feeling of anger or annoyance caused by being unable to do something.
goal	Something that you are trying to do or achieve.
grammar	The rules of how words are used in a language.
guarantee	A promise that something will be or will happen as stated.
guilt	A feeling of shame or regret as a result of bad conduct.
habit	A settled tendency or usual manner of behavior.
human right	A basic right that many societies believe every person should have.
humble	Not thinking of yourself as better than other people.
innovation	A new idea, method, or device.
inspiration	Something that moves someone to act, create, or feel an emotion.

interact	To talk or do things with other people.
intimidate	To make timid or fearful.
judgment	An opinion or decision that is based on careful thought.
manage	To take care of and make decisions about (someone's time, money, etc.).
maturity	The quality or state of being mature; especially full development.
media	The system and organizations of communication through which information is spread to a large number of people.
memory	The power or process of reproducing or recalling what has been learned and retained.
mindfulness	The practice of maintaining a nonjudgmental state of heightened or complete awareness of one's thoughts, emotions, or experiences.
mind-numbing	Very dull or boring.
motivation	The condition of being eager to act or work.
nutrition	The act or process of nourishing or being nourished.
opinion	Belief stronger than impression and less strong than positive knowledge.
opportunity	A favorable combination of circumstances, time, and place.
paper trail	Documents (such as financial records) from which a person's actions may be traced or opinions learned.
perspective	The ability to understand what is important and what isn't.
politics	The art or science of government.
ponder	To think about.
punctuation	The act or practice of inserting standardized marks or signs in written matter to clarify the meaning.
realistic	Ready to see things as they really are and to deal with them sensibly.
relationship	The state of interaction between two or more people, groups, or countries.
resolution	The final solving of a problem.
respect	To consider worthy of high regard.
retirement	Withdrawal of one's position or occupation or from active working life.
schedule	A written or printed list of things and the times when they will be done.
setback	A slowing of progress.
stress	A state of mental tension and worry caused by problems in your life, work, etc.
therapist	A person specializing in treating disorders or injuries of the body or mind, especially in ways that do not involve drugs and surgery.
trait	A quality that makes one person or thing different from another.
trust	To place confidence in someone or something.
valid	Based on truth or fact.

Further Reading

Brown, Brené. *Daring Greatly: How the Courage to Be Vulnerable Transforms the Way We Live, Love, Parent, and Lead.* New York: Avery, 2012.

Brukner, Lauren. *The Kids' Guide to Staying Awesome and in Control: Simple Stuff to Help Children Regulate Their Emotions and Senses.* Philadelphia: Jessica Kingsley Publishers, 2014.

Nelson, Robin. *Am I a Good Friend? A Book About Trustworthiness (Show Your Character).* Minneapolis: Lerner Publishing Group, 2014.

Willink, Jocko. *Way of the Warrior Kid: From Wimpy to Warrior the Navy SEAL Way.* New York: Feiwel and Friends, 2017.

Internet Resources

http://kidshealth.org/en/teens A "safe, private place" for teens and adolescents looking for accurate and actionable information about topics that matter, including self-esteem, sexual health, and mental well-being.

http://self-compassion.org/ A website that explores the research and work of psychologist Dr. Kristin Neff. Find resources on what self-compassion is, exercises to build your self-compassion, and guided meditations to help develop your compassionate practice.

https://www.dosomething.org/us Connect with millions of other teens and young adults from around the world to make a positive local or global impact. Visitors to this website can volunteer for a cause, join a civil-action campaign, and more.

https://www.projectknow.com/research/adolescent-teen-resources/ Education is the first step to prevention. This website offers great resources to kids, teens, and parents alike on how to talk about and seek help for issues around alcohol and drug use among the youth population.

Organizations to Contact

Boys and Girls Clubs of America
1275 Peachtree Street NE
Atlanta, GA 30309-3506
Phone: 404-487-5700
Website: https://www.bgca.org

Boys and Girls Clubs of Canada
400-2005 Sheppard Avenue East
Toronto, Ontario M2J 5B4
Phone: 905-477-7272
Fax: 416-640-5331
Website: https://www.bgccan.com/en/

Canada World Youth
2330 Notre-Dame Street West, Suite 300
Montreal, Quebec, H3J 1N4
Phone: 514-931-3526
Email: info@cwy-jcm.org
Website: http://canadaworldyouth.org

National Association for Self-Esteem
4352 Via Esperanza
Santa Barbara, CA 93110
Phone: 805-963-6501
Fax: 805-832-6092
Email: betty@selfesteem.org
Website: http://www.selfesteem.org

Index

Picture Credits

All images in this book are in the public domain or have been supplied under license by © Shutterstock.com. The publisher credits the following images as follows: page 12: Maythee Voran, page 13: Klauscook, page 16: J Stone, © Dreamstime/page 6 above: Brianna Hunter, page 6 below: Rawpixelimages, page 7 above: Andrea de Martin, page 7 below Vladyslav Starozhylov.

To the best knowledge of the publisher, all images not specifically credited are in the public domain. If any image has been inadvertently uncredited, please notify the publisher, so that credit can be given in future printings.

Video Credits

Page 14 Attitude Is Altitude: http://x-qr.net/1Fd5, page 25: BuzzFeedVideo http://x-qr.net/1Cui, page 31 Noah Hammond Tyrrell: http://x-qr.net/1FQx, page 36 BRIGHT SIDE: http://x-qr.net/1F7g, page 48 Charisma on Command: http://x-qr.net/1DWK, page 55 BRIGHT SIDE: http://x-qr.net/1DAN

About the Author

Sarah Smith is a freelance writer currently living and working in the Boston area. She is also a board-certified Doctor of Physical Therapy, licensed by the Commonwealth of Massachusetts. She attended Boston University, where she earned both her doctorate and, as an undergraduate, a bachelor of science in health studies.

Sarah has been writing for her entire life, and first became a published author at age fourteen, when she began contributing to a weekly column for her local newspaper. Since beginning her freelance writing career in earnest in 2014, Sarah has written over 1,500 articles and books. Her work covers a broad range of topics, including psychology and relationships, as well as physical and mental health.

Additionally, she has over fifteen years of professional experience working with typically developing and special-needs children, along with their families, in a variety of settings, including schools, pediatric hospitals, and youth-group fitness programs. She spent over thirteen years working as a private nanny and babysitter for families in both her hometown of Yarmouth, Maine, as well as in and around the great city of Boston. Sarah also has experience tutoring and leading teens and young adults as part of a variety of clinical internship programs for physical therapy.